MW00915661

GOLD RUSH!

A Kid's Guide To Techatticup Gold Mine, Eldorado Canyon, Nevada

PHOTOGRAPHY BY JOHN D. WEIGAND
POETRY BY PENELOPE DYAN

Bellissima Publishing, LLC
Jamul, California
www.bellissimapublishing.com

copyright © 2010 by Penny D. Weigand and John D. Weigand

All rights reserved. No part of this book may be
reproduced or transmitted in any form or by any means,
electronic or mechanical, including photocopying,
recording, or by any other means, or by any information or
storage retrieval system, without permission from the publisher.

ISBN 978-1-935630-11-1

First Edition

To The
Kids of RVA
& Adam
2010

For Kids Who Love Adventures!
And For Parents Who Love to Go On Adventures With them!

Gold Rush!

Bellissima Publishing, LLC

Introduction

The Nelson and Eldorado Canyon areas were home to ancient Puebloan, Paiutes and Mojave Indians who lived in peace there for hundred of years. In 1775, Spaniards arrived looking for gold. They settled at the mouth of the Colorado River and called it Eldorado. However, they missed the rich gold veins beneath the canyon's flanks, and found silver and there was not enough silver to make mining worthwhile, and so they left. By 1861 miners discovered the Salvage Vein about five miles up from the Colorado River, a rich, vertically stacked ribbon of gold running through a steep ridge along one side of the canyon. Several miners formed the Techatticup Mine through a series of shady dealings. The name is the Paiute Indian word for hungry, a term heard by early settlers and said by the starving Indians inhabiting the dry hills. The Techatticup Gold Mine was once owned by Senator George Hearst of California, father of William Randolph Hearst, the famous publisher. The history of the area is fascinating. Where else can you hear about prospectors who were Civil War deserters, gunfights over gold, daily killings and other acts so despicable even law enforcement refused to come from a mere 200 miles away? There was virtually no law in Eldorado Canyon, and the Techatticup Mine was in the middle of it all!

Now owned by a family whose five sons have cleared tunnels through the mine and have found and uncovered even more of its history, this is the place to be and see American history and how a part of it was formed. So take a tour through the pages of this book with photographer John D. Weigand, and award winning author and poet, Penelope Dyan and see what they saw when they explored this fascinating place!

Gold Rush!

Bellissima Publishing, LLC

GOLD RUSH!

A Kid's Guide To Techatticup Gold Mine, Eldorado Canyon, Nevada

PHOTOGRAPHY BY JOHN D. WEIGAND
POETRY BY PENELOPE DYAN

See the Techatticup Gold Mine Company Store
restored where it once stood,
in a very different kind of a neighborhood.
This was once a neighborhood full of wantonness and greed,
where lawless men serving themselves was their only need.
It was full of deserters from both sides of the Civil War!
They feuded right there as they'd fought before.
And when all has been said and told,
these lawless men were here for one reason,
and that reason was Gold!

It all began about eighteen hundred and sixty one,
In the mountains above the Colorado River in harsh desert sun.
Now Hollywood producers shoot movies there.
And about the former lawlessness they just do not care.

And if you take a look in the old company store,
You'll find history on its walls, and you'll find even more!

You can see a very old safe, an old telephone and stuff. . .

And you can see rattlesnake headbands,
and if that's not enough. . .

You can see alien skulls presumedly from outer space.
They're right there next to the bobcat, a perfect place!

There is a water tower.

There is a restored barn.
There are those who tell history weaving a wonderful yarn.

This property is where people who own this place now live.
And as to our country's history, they have a lot to give!
The property was dedicated in 2001,
And the restoration is not yet all done.
But there certainly is a lot to see,
and the Techatticup Mine is the place to be!

TECHATTICUP MINE

THE TECHATTICUP MINE, LOCATED IN 1861, WAS THE MOST IMPORTANT MINE IN EL DORADO CANYON. IT PRODUCED MILLIONS OF DOLLARS IN GOLD ORE, AND WAS ORIGINALLY SERVED BY STEAMBOATS ON THE COLORADO RIVER. THE MINE'S NAME IS TAKEN FROM TWO PAIUTE WORDS MEANING "HUNGRY" OR "BREAD".

TWO OF NEVADA'S MOST FAMOUS RENEGADE INDIANS LIVED IN THE CANYON; AHVOTE, WHO KILLED FIVE VICTIMS, AND QUEHO, WHO KILLED OVER TWENTY PEOPLE. NEAR THIS SPOT, QUEHO KILLED HIS LAST VICTIM, MAUDE DOUGLAS, IN 1919, AND SUCCESSFULLY ELUDED SHERIFF'S POSSES.

DEDICATED SEPTEMBER 24, 2000
QUEHO POSSE CHPT. #191 OF THE ANCIENT & HONORABLE ORDER
E CLAMPUS VITUS

This is the watchman's shack where the watchman would stay,
and where the watchman could sleep when night overtook day.

And this is the blacksmith's shop. . .
where the blacksmith's work just did not stop.

And here is the very old, old mine,
where you can go inside and even more history find!
Yes, here it stand's, a history door. . .
just waiting for you and another to explore!

And once you go through that old mine door,
There are so many cleared tunnels you can explore.
It's dark and scary, and you can bet,
you need to watch your every step!
And once you get really deep inside,
from the scary ghosts you cannot hide!

Here is the canary cage where a canaries once breathed air.
And if a canary fell dead, the miners got right out of there.
Because when a canary died in here, it meant the air was bad.
And so to get out of there, the miners were glad.

And here is a bucket and some other mining tools
that the old time miners also used.
It was also very, very, very dark,
and lanterns and candles gave light's spark.

And here is a replica of dear old Ed,
who got a stake right through his head. . .
He was right there pounding in his stake,
when he made a huge mistake.
And boom, his stake into his head flew,
and there was absolutely nothing that old Ed could do!

Here is a tunnel going into the mountain deep,
where sometimes at night the miners would sleep.
They worked the mines hard, or so I am told,
in the hope of finding a vein of gold.

And here is another tunnel too!
You can see the mountain sides the miners dug through!
They say this is a ghostly place,
haunted by ungodly men who died in disgrace.
They were deserters, thieves, and unlawful men,
who in death must relive their sins all over again.
So if you happen to go inside and see a ghost,
Please run like crazy. . .it's not your host!

A very high platform walk forms a brand new floor,
giving you one more place that you can explore!
Because there are tunnels in this mountain all the way through,
there is a lot that you can see and do.
And here is the very most important part. . .
Here in this place history does become art;
because everything is set out especially,
for kids like you to come and see.
And oh the tales the tour guide will tell. . .
because he knows this place so well.
So take a look in the mine's general store,
and see everything there is in here to explore.
And when all is said and done,
You will say learning wild west history is lots of fun!

The End

Always look for the light at the end of the tunnel!

LaVergne, TN USA
10 June 2010
185757LV00002B